Ameriphobia

The Unfounded Fear of America

By

Robert George

Ameriphobia – The Unfounded Fear of America

By Robert George

Copyright 2017 Robert George

Printed in the United States of America

robertgeorgeDT@aol.com

ISBN-13: 978-1542604802

ISBN-10: 154260480X

Library of Congress Control Number 2017902463

Table of Contents

Overview

Americans are constantly being told to tolerate people from different cultures; and, especially, not to fear people from Islamic countries. The term Islamophobia is used to stigmatize and "guilt" Americans into believing that their fears about terrorism are a latent hatred of Islamic believers. Many conservative Americans are thought to be bigoted and irrational when it comes to their attitudes about race and religion. Conservatives are thought to be prejudiced against people of other religions because their cause is that of Christ rather than Allah.

Yet, many Americans have a deep suspicion of Muslims solely because of the way the 9/11 terrorists infiltrated our country. Are such fears rational or bigoted? This is a clearly important question. How do we define rational thinking when it is known that Islam has among its members several people openly desirous of destroying America and its values?

To understand this, we must develop some clear facts:

1. America did not deserve to be attacked on 9/11.

2. The ideas of anti-capitalism animated the 9/11 destroyers.
3. Islam has an Anti-American, anti-secular set of prejudices.
4. Many Muslims hold those prejudices while others do not.

Let us look at these facts more thoroughly:

1. America did not deserve to be attacked on 9/11.
   The basis of the idea that America deserved what it got on 9/11/2001 is the false notion that the USA represents an evil culture that should be punished by the world and its moral agents. Why is this advocated by so many people?

   Commerce is a normal human activity. Why should any religion think of it as base and sinful? America is the preeminent example of a nation that fosters and engages in commerce in the world. This activity can only be good if people are free to make their own trade decisions. It is freedom that provides the incentive toward excellence and mutual trade to mutual advantage. This is true even in religious dictatorships. People must trade to survive.

Properly, no ideology can define commerce as an evil activity. This is because moral choices are effective only to the extent that they are indeed moral; they benefit the actor. Commerce can only be based upon the ability of men to make the good decisions that result in their self-interest being accomplished. There can be no other motive for commerce outside of the need of men to trade and benefit their own lives.

Yet, there are people who believe that commerce is evil. Why? What is it about commerce that some consider to be immoral?

The earliest examples of this anti-commerce view come to us from ancient times. The prehistoric Greeks appear to have built their world upon conquest and plunder (see the Iliad). Their gods were the planets who ruled man and the world by war and religion. They held to a metaphysical, epistemological and ethical dualism where the gods and spirits were deemed superior to men. This view relegated men to the activities of living like the gods lived by emulating them in their everyday living. The individual earned a place in heaven through loyalty to god and obedience.

Metaphysical dualism divides reality between the spiritual world (where the gods live) and the material world where man lives. Epistemological dualism divides concepts into the mystical (which men access intrinsically) and the real, which is (supposedly) outside of man's comprehension and, finally, moral dualism divides morality into doing what god wants and doing what the individual wants (which is considered base and evil). It is logical then, from this foundation that anything done by the individual for himself is by necessity inferior to anything done for god. Within such an intellectual climate, then the secular (without religion) is the immoral. This is the view of many religions including both Christianity and Islam.

With mysticism comes collectivism and the idea that god wants man to live in collective enclaves of unknowing and unthinking automatons who do only that which is verified by the group. Where mysticism is the sacrifice of the mind, collectivism is the sacrifice of the body for the sake of keeping the group alive.

Since commerce, capitalism and trade are all secular activities (they must be secular because they require reason and deal with the real world) and since the secular is associated with sin and doing wrong, anti-capitalism can only be part of a "total" way of life; one that rejects wholesale anything that would derive from reason. Here we have Islam, Christianity, Marxism, anarchy, asceticism and self-disdain. Anti-secularism/anti-capitalism, then, is the philosophy of anti-man. Islam is merely one example of an anti-man philosophy. It is not the only such philosophy.

Secularism is an enticing idea because it represents freedom and individual morality. Some forms of religion even allow secular elements to exist side-by-side with religion. In this way, religious people can sometimes enjoy the fruits of secularism while adhering to mystical ideas. In fact, there are some Muslims who are secular and business oriented, although the main thrust of Islam is anti-secular.

For many religious radicals, secularism is more than just evil, it is the cause of all evil. This is because their religion is constantly beating a drum against individuality and individual initiative. The Muslim radicals want to destroy secularism and replace it with the Muslim religion – in the name of justice, peace, love and faith. To accomplish this, fascistic forms of oppression against the secular west become religiously appropriate.

Another secular activity is the creation of arts and crafts. We know from early times (according to Herodotus) that craftsmen were considered a lowly class in Egypt and other nations surrounding the Mediterranean. The upper classes were comprised of nobles who had earned their positions through heredity. These were the warrior classes who were sponsored by the god of war. These men were entrusted to be of service to the king and to protect his power. Warrior cultures grew up admiring these men and the king granted successful warriors land, hereditary power and even slaves to serve them. The lowly craftsman, on the other hand, was fortunate if he became a gift from the king to the nobleman.

Under this formula, the craftsman was a doer of things in the real world and hence inferior. Yet, wealthy warriors, administrators and noblemen were rich (in the real world), enjoyed their luxuries and pleasures, precisely because of the slaves they mastered, the works they created, the meals they cooked and the palaces they built. The craftsman was the secret weapon of a society that disdained him.

When a religion declares war on anything that involves the real world; it descends intellectually into a vast expanse of hatred of the good. It looks to put out all the lights of independence and seeks to make of every individual a willing slave in the name of god.

When living in the world is considered the height of decadence; when dressing western (provocatively) in clothing that reveals the body, religious judges rule that men are descending into a world of blasphemy against god. This anti-secularism is an attack on life, choice, volition, individual accomplishment and even happiness. Is it any wonder that some factions of religion want to convert the world by means of religious law and even destroy the "monuments" to decadence, pride and blasphemy?

This is certainly a culture clash. When thousands of people have declared war upon a made-up blasphemy, we are going to have to make a choice between rational survival and irrational man-hatred. If we agree that commerce is sinful, that America is evil, then we are going to have to choose Islam (or some such religion) as our system of ideas. And we must do what they demand; which is to sacrifice everything for those ideas including our minds and our lives.

Consider that Islam takes the spirit, Allah, to represent the height of purity. It's attitude towards women is expressly based upon the idea that women, unclothed, present men with the choice of "Jezebel" the harlot. On the other hand, when she is fully covered, fully unsexual, she is the slave to men whose only goals are to keep them down; to ensure that they are not allowed to tempt them with their worldly bodies – all in the name of remaining pure and sinless. The upshot is that human beings are impure by nature and an ethereal God is the only pure agent in the universe.

So, for these Muslims, all women, especially the harlots of the west (normal women who dress provocatively), who do whatever they want, who knowingly tempt men with the exposure of their bodies are the repositories of evil. The west which sells them their clothing, their perfumes, their nylons their lipstick and cosmetics and even enables them to have surgery that enhances their sexual appeal, must surely be the den of Satan. The west, for them, is the Great Satan and it must be destroyed totally to create a world of piety and love for god. Indeed, "the guerdon of all praise" in this anti-world world is the descent into the un-living and un-feeling. To be this kind of Muslim is to forsake everything that exists and to worship something "in heaven".

How can we answer such devotion to the

sanctity of the spirit when so many of us worship our own spirit? What makes ours different? This brings up the question of the value of a secular society.

2. The ideas of anti-capitalism animated the 9/11 destroyers.

   Ameriphobia is more real than Islamophobia. All one must do is identify the principles that make up Ameriphobia and one will see a much larger phobia of which the proponents of Islamophobia are a part. Indeed, those who proclaim that America is Islamophobic base their antagonism upon false premises that have nothing to do with reality. Starting with religion's war against the individual and profit, moving to Karl Marx and his critique of capitalism and then combining these into the anti-secularism of Islamic radicals, we arrive at a wholly false view of the world that removes the advocates of Islamic violence from credibility. As mystics, they are not able to see the inapplicability of their concept of "religious truth". As anti-Americans, they possess false notions of the value and applicability of capitalism and free markets. As moralists, they have no moral base upon which to found their antagonism to secular (non-religious) society.

The source of Ameriphobia is predominantly Karl Marx. Marx's critique of capitalism is reputed to spell out certain flaws in capitalism that socialism is designed to correct. Deriving his views from Christianity, Marx followed suit and declared profit-seeking and production to be worldly, secular and evil as such. These views are found in several prominent religions and are based upon a general antipathy toward commerce, profit and usury. In fact, the critique of capitalism in Karl Marx's writings parallels the critiques of America expressed by terrorists and many radical Imams today.

These anti-capitalist myths can be expressed by the following statements:

1. Capitalism is individualistic rather than collectivist (collectivism is considered (without reason) to be superior to individualism)

2. Capitalism is inefficient and socialism is efficient (which is untrue)

3. Capitalism is Imperialistic (which is arrived at by falsely attaching colonialism and

mercantilism to capitalism)

4. Capitalism is decadent and immoral (which is based upon the mind-body split that sees anything that involves reality as evil, dirty and base)

I will not go into the debates over these critiques of capitalism here but I will state that these four statements are false. They are based upon a fundamental idea that self-interest is evil. They are repeated constantly all over the world and especially in American universities where many Muslims come to be educated. They create a massive prejudice among average people all over the world toward America and American businesspeople. They are expressed in American movies by American actors and they create prejudice against anything American. They justify countless unnecessary and restrictive regulations of capitalism and they justify and animate countless violent anti-capitalist and anti-American groups around the world. These groups and ideas poison the world against self-interest, justify dictatorships and foment hate and destruction. The false Marxist critique of capitalism has devastated and impoverished the 20th Century and stands poised to destroy our economies today. The existence of this critique implicates the leftists in America today as destroyers of freedom and the killers of men.

If you read the arguments of CAIR, Usama bin Ladin, OWS, anti-capitalist Christians, President Obama, Van Jones and others on the left, you will hear these arguments openly, some advocating violence, others advocating government expansion.

The anti-capitalists don't want you to know that their solution to capitalism is worse than capitalism. They talk about what's wrong with capitalism and what they are doing to fix it, but ignore the fact that what's wrong with capitalism is that they are interfering with it.

3. Islam has an anti-secular set of prejudices. These prejudices come primarily from the anti-secular, pro-mysticism mindset of religion but they are exacerbated by a fawning left establishment in American universities as well as the influences left over from Anti-American propaganda that was introduced into the middle east by the Soviets who sought to infiltrate Arab countries during the cold war.

4. Many Muslims hold those prejudices while others do not. The combination of anti-secularism and anti-capitalism make for a lethal ideology that is based upon hatred of America and assigning secularism to the realm of Satan. Many individual Muslims, even many who are not violent or intent on harming people, still hold those prejudices against American society. It is these prejudices that make up what I call Ameriphobia. This is the fear that Americans will exploit, disenfranchise and even kill Muslims for the sake of oil or profit.

The list of fallacies held according to this view include many. Among them is the idea that commerce represents theft of land, natural resources or money and that Americans have no moral scruples when it comes to "raiding" the riches of other nations. That such activities are not theft but mutual trade is not important for those who hate the very idea of doing anything for the sake of profit.

Why does the left instinctively oppose individual rights? To answer this question, we need to examine the fundamental views of the progressive movement. Not only did the progressive movement come out of the socialist left and Marxism, it has brought with it all the Marxist anti-capitalism that it could.

As pragmatists, progressives think that the only practical approach is re-distribution, government coercion and economic manipulation. This false philosophy of government leaves progressives incapable of advancing policies that produce abundance and moral living. This exposes the medieval aspect of the left's philosophy of government. It is not a philosophy of "hope" because it seeks the destruction of hope in one half of its population in order to lift the burden of living from the other half. One cannot have hope in a society that makes the individual a slave.

The left believes, as did the Church, that profit is evil and that everything possible should be done to restrict and limit it. Scratch a progressive and you'll find a medievalist who holds that commerce is done by shysters who do business not to trade value for value

but to cheat people out of their money. The prejudice that the left expresses toward business people is the telltale sign of a medieval approach to economics and politics. In this sense, they have more in common with Islamic radicals who would kill Americans because they hate individual autonomy and secularly-based freedoms.

Today's progressives don't have the courage to follow their communist fellow-travelers by shedding their own blood on the streets but you can count on them to give mealy-mouthed lip service to the anti-capitalism of Islamic murderers and to argue that Muslims are the victims of American imperialism who are justified in hating America. They want us to "understand" the radicals and see why they are angry at us but they will never stand for the right of free individuals to live without the fascist control of Sharia Law.

If there is any group of Americans who are more responsible for terrorism and the growing violence of Islamic radicals in the world, it is American progressive college professors. The American progressive movement has liberated Islamic murderers and anti-capitalists to do their crimes. Rather than call schizophrenic delusions for what they are, they prefer to brand the radicals as sane and American freedom as oppressive. As collectivists, they would defend the "rights" of the most murderous collectivists of any ethnic variety rather than declare the individual free of collective binds.

A Secular Society

The sanctity of the spirit is the essential religious issue. But the essential question for man is the nature of the spiritual in man's life. Answering this question has consumed innumerable volumes throughout history. Muslims, other anti-westerners and anti-secularists worship a spirit that is considered to be the height of all purity and goodness. Yet, this spirit is ephemeral, unseen, and the moral system "He" espouses is total self-sacrifice of mind, body and soul. And this is considered good and unquestionable.

Either we take the spiritual seriously and absorb it into our thinking or we dismiss the concept completely. One could say that man is spiritual by nature; that he should celebrate his spirituality as part of his psychological makeup. But this assumes that being spiritual is something good – and, in fact, we cannot make that assumption without question.

On the other hand, when we practice moral precepts in the world of real things, when we seek rational living, we must relegate god to the status of irrelevant. We must build our world around things (that are not evil by nature), entities (that can be shown to be real and beneficial to man), ideas (that can be validated and shown to be moral), principles (that work in the real world) and concepts (whose definitions help the individual live for his own needs and which are effective in helping him achieve survival and understanding).

The ancient Greeks were the first near-secular society. Some of their most prominent thinkers sought a "real-world" answer to questions of cosmology. They were confronted by the various believers in the Gods who saw the universe as managed by spiritual participants in the lives of men. Many Greeks thought it prudent to participate in the various sacrificial rites which were common among them. These rites were intent on paying homage to the gods and living according to their precepts. Even Plato, the father of mysticism, often mentioned them in his writings.

Earlier, Homer, the preeminent poet of the Greeks wrote of the gods and their participation in the Trojan War. Here the gods appear like politicians manipulating events in the background by talking directly to human warriors and even slinging arrows themselves as warriors in the battles. Some of the human warriors are described as semi-divine humans with great powers who participated on the side of both Greeks and Trojans.

This war, in a sense, was a metaphor for modern man who had been so influenced by the gods that he saw them in everything he did. The devastations which were happening throughout the world set this mystical framework into the minds of men and gave them a central mythology around which to build their cosmologies and the moral premises they derived from them.

The division of the mystical and the rational was represented by essentially two groups of Greeks. The first group, the Platonists were the precursors of every religion that followed. They accepted the existence of the gods and they thought of them as moral agents. The second group were the Aristotelians who were (with some exceptions) the precursors of secular society which, over time, rejected the gods as living agents, relegated them to the world of the spirit and saw a focus on reality as their founding principle.

The Platonists believed in another dimension which was the home of all essential concepts including the gods. This concept prevailed throughout hundreds of religions, each with varying doctrines. Islam was only one of those doctrines.

The turn which man made at this time was indicative of a major psychological trauma. Somehow, primitive man began to fear his natural environment and this corrupted the process of knowledge acquisition for survival. Where he should have looked at reality, he invented spirits, demons and gods to intervene on his behalf and to annihilate his enemies.

Those men who accepted the existence of the "other dimension" became the mystics and religionists. Starting with the "mystery religions" and moving progressively toward monotheism, these people developed a "personal" relationship with a spiritual entity which, as defined today, did not exist.

Islam came into being after the Christian development of the Jewish monotheistic conception. Reacting to these developments, during the 7th century A.D., Islam developed a similar theocracy based upon their god Allah who came from the mind of a leader named Muhammad. The combination of religion and politics was the opposite development from what had taken place in the Greek (more secular) world.

Eventually, the secular approach led men away from mysticism and postulated a world view away from religion. This was the birth of modern science and a view of reality that focused on existence rather than another dimension.

Christianity and Islam became opponents in the struggle for dominance in Europe and Africa. Both became "political" in the sense that they believed in using force to expand their "domains" and they both went to war against each other. This war was essentially a stalemate but during this period we saw the development of theocratic monarchies which virtually dictated to their followers how they should act and what they should believe.

Then came the Enlightenment (which was an outgrowth of the secular Aristotelian view that reality was knowable). During this period, the west was subjected to a growing focus on reality and there was a muted intellectual development that challenged the dominance of Christianity. This challenge was most noticeable in science where a host of intellectuals began the reconsideration of the nature of the solar system and this challenge resulted in a repudiation of the view that the earth was the center of the universe. Intellectuals such as Locke, Bacon and others began the creation of secularism which was an effort to remove God as the center of all knowledge and to replace him with a view that the universe functions based on laws that had to be discovered by man.

This gave rise to the geniuses who began the quest for knowledge and culminated in an effort to remove God as the source of knowledge. Some intellectuals (notably Locke), although Christian in most respects, had to couch their ideas within a blanket of religion (because of the power of the Church) but insinuated logic and reason at the same time. This development led to the concept of individual rights and the right of man to think for himself and act on the basis of his reasoning ability.

In the Muslim world, with some exceptions, this emphasis on the secular was not as pronounced in spite of the fact that it was Arabic intellectuals who had resurrected the writings of Aristotle and other Greeks. Over time, the dominant Muslim factions continued their theocratic bent and opened the field to uncompromising mysticism as the only repository of purity and good.

What made Christianity and Islam so powerful? It was the fact that they were both political and religious. Both religions took on the sense of being the only source of moral guidance based upon faith in the existence of God as well the combining of religion with politics. Both religions held the ancient view that the gods were real and their pronouncements were sacred. They held that moral action based upon mystical (rationalistic) premises was the only right way. This gave the leaders of each religion, during the middle ages, the power to dictate and force people to do "the right thing".

With this legacy of dictatorial power for both Christianity and Islam, how did they diverge? What caused one religion to become benign and rights-respecting and the other to become fascistic and war-like?

The answer has to do with the advent of secularism in Europe and the absence of secularism in much of the Islamic world. In Europe, the concept of individual rights (via Locke) led to the development of intellectual movements that fought against government power and the encroachments of government into the lives of people. As I have indicated elsewhere, creative man was always looking for a way to reduce and/or eliminate the power of monarchical government over his life and choices. Eventually, this led to the provision in the U.S. Constitution of the Bill of Rights which limited government and restricted its power to intervene in peoples' lives. The concept of a separation between religion and state removed religion from government and forbade the government from making any laws related to religion. This not only created "religious freedom" but it also liberated people of all religions as well as people of no religion. At this point, it became possible for people to live without religion and to base their personal and private decisions on the requirements of reality.

In short, because of the demand for individual rights, Christianity had to reform itself and become a new version of the old tyranny. It had to respect the rights of all people to think and believe as they saw fit and this factor eliminated the need of the various religions to fight each other and especially to use government to gain political advantage over religious opponents. A life without religion became possible and, more importantly, this condition was seen as good (positive). There was no aura of evil and sin associated with secularism.

The outgrowth of the freedoms liberated by the Bill of Rights was the growth and development of objective laws based upon logic rather than the pronouncements of priests and/or religious morality. Economically, this created capitalism and made it possible for individuals to live morally through the judgment of their individual minds. There could be no evil associated with capitalism because people were free to make their own decisions and decide for themselves. These were, in effect, moral decisions. They not only improved economies but also eliminated the centuries-old admonitions against sex, gambling, cohabitation and other actions that the Church had proscribed.

A secular life was not considered a sign of evil but a sign of independence. What Christianity had once seen as a den of sin, secular society saw as a den of individualism and of individual self-assertion. People became happier, cleaner, better dressed and affluent – and this created pride. This was what it meant to be an American.

On the other hand, the world of Islam went through no such Enlightenment. This is not to say that Islam today has not been reformed. The influence of capitalism and global trade has caused some Muslim nations and some forms of Islam to reform in order to benefit from the economic security that capitalism creates. And it is also true that there are a small number of radical Christians who have every intention of reinstituting religious control over government.

There are essentially two attacks on the secularism of the west by elements within Islam. The first is Sharia Law and the second is jihadism.

Sharia Law

Sharia Law is based upon religious prophesy. It is not based upon reality or the requirements of survival. Sharia Law is a formal legal system based upon the interpretation of the Koran and the Hadith which are taken as the thoughts of Mohammed. Although interpretations can differ, the key point is that Sharia Law is derived from the word of Allah as understood by Mohammad the Prophet and subsequent other representatives of the religion.

As interpretation of Allah, Sharia law is rationalistic in nature; that is, it is based upon mystical sources not reality. As such, it is based upon opinions of moral law rather than rational considerations. This rationalism is a characteristic of virtually all moral systems derived from god or religious systems. In short, it is invalid as a guide for living in society. Additionally, it is the source of many violations of the rights of individuals and leads to much cruelty and harm to individuals.

For instance, when a group of men decides that god's law demands the stoning of women who engage in adultery, they are not adhering to reality but to a view of sex that sees pleasure as evil and despicable. To rationalize such actions as being demanded by god is merely to find an unjustified excuse to do harm to women who do not deserve any punishment whatsoever. Their choices of sexual partners is not for anyone to judge. A rational society would view morality as properly based upon individual choice and reason and it leaves people free to make their own choices.

Sharia Law can be considered a form of torts. Torts are laws that prescribe a specific punishment for specific acts. If you violate one of them, then the punishment is clear. But the key wrong of this is that these "torts" are derived from ancient texts and are extracted from them as an organizing principle of society. In this sense, they are political rather than merely moral. They are a form of social control prescribed by religious authorities (as representatives of god). They cover not only political but also personal issues as well as faith. They represent an imposition that is implied in the very idea that there is such a thing as a singular correct religion. It is implied that Sharia laws are divinely written laws with zero-tolerance. What we in a secular country would consider theocracy, the imposition of religious tenets, the true believing Muslims consider Sharia Law to be the unquestionable word of God.

Although Sharia Law has been practiced in many nations, there is no nation that strictly follows only

Sharia Law. Some nations include laws derived from Sharia but also have full legal systems outside of Sharia.

Certainly, it is true that if someone believes in a religion and the laws derived from it, they want their government to adhere to religious laws. But there are societies in which religion is relegated to the status of the unscientific. In such societies, principles are integrated around the idea that everyone has the right and responsibility to do as he pleases within the principles of civil behavior. Burying a woman in the ground and then stoning her to death is not civilized behavior.

Another example of a religious society (or a theology) was created by the Hebrews who escaped from the slavery of Egypt. They had founded a new religion that was essentially based upon Egyptian religious precepts and the new God who had just liberated them. Moses, their founder, wrote the Ten Commandments, not merely for the sake of worshipping their singular God, but also as the foundation of their legal code.

Sharia Law would be dangerous for America. Because our nation adheres to principles such as individual rights, our fundamentality requires consistency and deliberation. Our punishments are civilized (without also being cruel and excessive) whereas Sharia Law countenances stonings and cutting-off-of-hands, acts that are barbaric for a secular people.

It is not likely that rights-respecting citizens will ever accept such brutal practices as a means of discouraging crime. This vicious cruelty in the name of god must surely prove that god has no place in civilized jurisprudence. Piety and belief cannot possibly justify such brutality.

"What causes people to believe?" "What makes them decide to live their life according to a system of faith rather than a system of reason?" "Is there something superior in the concept of faith that makes people think their lives are better because of it?" "In what way do they gage the idea of living a better life through religion?" "Should religious people be forced by secular principles to reform their religions and put them in compliance with individual rights?"

These are important questions that hint at the crisis in mysticism today. It is mysticism that must answer these questions and it is mystics who must decide whether they will live according to barbarous thoughts or elevate their thinking in order to live in modern secular societies.

There is nothing in mysticism that makes it a

superior mode of thinking and/or understanding. In fact, mysticism is a negation of reality and man's means of ascertaining truth (reason). There is nothing that makes it better than reason and rationality. Piety, as an outgrowth of mysticism, is essentially a cover-up of the fact that mysticism demands the persecution and punishment of anyone who does not adhere to its tenets.

Jihadism

In fact, mysticism, as irrationality, gives evil men the opportunity to justify their hateful and murderous acts by pretending to be seeking the good. Monsters can do anything they want so long as they couch it as piety and love of god.

The monsters within Islam insinuate themselves into our lives by coming to our country and taking advantage of our tolerance with deadly result. Are terrorists lurking among us still, acting westernized yet working to kill us? Are some of the people who immigrate to America today "sleepers" who will do the same as the 9/11 terrorists?

Jihadism is a form of warfare. The best term to describe it, in modern terms, is that it is a "neologism", a form of logic separate from the traditional forms of classical (logical) reasoning. A neologism contains its own "truth" that cannot be understood by those not adhering to its premises. This inoculates the jihadists from criticism (if you accept the premises of neologism).

If one analyzes jihadism carefully, one will find that the term neologism is a dodge. It is a way of putting it outside the scrutiny of anyone who is not a jihadist. In other words, their logic is true for them and not true for you; therefore, you cannot judge it. You can't even walk in their shoes and understand their lives because of your own western prejudices.

Jihadism, as a neologism, is nothing more than another form of violent revolution. It was Marx and Engels who preached that Marxism was a neologism that western capitalists could not understand. In this way, they could justify violent acts of revolution against the west. They held that it was not possible for capitalists to understand revolutionary socialism and the best thing to do was to kill them in order to get on with building the new socialist world.

In fact, jihadism is based upon Marxism. As I have pointed out, the Marxists of the Soviet Union spent many decades fomenting violent revolution against "western elements" in the middle east. They taught that the property, the land, belonged to the people and that Americans were stealing "their" oil. They taught that the U.S.A. was exploiting them and trying to enslave them. They taught that violent revolution was necessary to kick the Americans out and send them home.

Jihadists tie themselves to Islam but the truth of the matter is that they are nothing more than criminals. As such, their struggle is not about creating a theocratic and pure religious government. They are not fighting for their people or to regain their rights as a people. This is all collectivist claptrap used to lure the unknowing into thinking that they are fighting for a cause. The true goal of jihadism is to institute gangsterism, gang warfare and fascism. As such, they are more closely tied to the German Nazis than any other group in history. This explains their anti-Jewish hatred and their unwillingness to work with or cooperate with any system that represents capitalism. Jihadists want to control everything and they will allow no "representative" form of government. They are the appointed of Allah and their neologism will never allow anyone to be their equal. You must either submit or die.

Hatred of America

I don't think our fear of being attacked again is unfounded. It is a genuine fear based upon the fact that many Americans have been killed by religious fanatics in the name of Islam. And I find it curious that we are told by many on the left that there is no terrorist threat, that the entire issue is stoked up by the right to create paranoia among us and generate political support for increased military and homeland security spending.

The terrorists among us were educated by religious leaders, men of God, who breathed venomous hatred toward Americans. We are told that this anti-American speech still takes place in many mosques in America. Is our generosity being taken advantage of again? No, we are told, we should realize that our fear of Islamic radicals is a sickness based on our past racist tendencies. Too many of us are Islamophobes, they tell us, and we have nothing to fear from terrorists.

Yet, the question I would ask is "Are we more afraid of them than they are afraid of us?" What makes so many in the Muslim world want to kill us? Is it their love of humanity or pure unadulterated hatred? Many in the left tell us it is not as simple as that; that there are many factors that contribute to the fear of Muslims, much of which is related to our latent and past racism toward blacks and other minorities. According to this view, our past and present racism is responsible for our unfounded views toward Muslims.

Notice that the left seldom acknowledges the evil of terrorism. This is because many of them see the genesis of terrorism in the foreign policies of western countries rather than as evil acts done to free and innocent people in the west. As anti-capitalists, they see capitalism as aggressive and exploitative of other countries. They tell us that when these other countries see how we "steal" their resources, they are moved to hate the west and retaliate. That retaliation takes the form of justified violent rebellion in order to be rid of our exploitation of them.

To understand these issues, I recently read a booklet published jointly by the Council on Islamic Relations (CAIR) and The University of Berkeley Center for Race and Gender entitled "'Same Hate, New Target' Islamophobia in the United States, January 2009, December 2010". This booklet provided an interesting perspective on the question of Islamophobia. In fact, it was more than merely interesting; it was frightening – not for what it revealed about Islamophobia but for what it revealed about Ameriphobia, the unfounded fear of America.

First, the article made no effort to scientifically document the existence of Islamophobia in America. There were several anecdotes about anti-Muslim incidents but much of that can be dismissed as unrepresentative of the clear majority of Americans. Just as you cannot cite a few instances of racism in America to prove racism among the vast majority, you cannot point to a few examples of anger directed at Muslims to indicate a general fear of Islam. It simply isn't accurate. But that doesn't stop the CAIR and Berkeley writers of this booklet.

For instance, CAIR's National Director, Mr. Nihad Awad, in his letter published in the article, calls Islamophobia "close-minded prejudice against or hatred of Islam and Muslims…"

This is a flawed definition of Islamophobia. Prejudice is not a phobia. Prejudice is making judgments about a certain person without having all the facts. A "phobia" is an irrational fear. And I submit that no one can provide a scientific study that definitively proves that Americans are irrationally afraid of Islam or that they are fundamentally racist.

What is the point of this definition if it defines nothing? Fear is usually aimed at a person or object that is a threat to one's life. Fear of having ourselves or our fellow Americans killed by terrorists is a real fear. But if you can call a rational fear a "phobia", you make a person question his fear while you do nothing to alleviate it. You create moral paralysis; you make it impossible for the rationally fearful person to do anything about his fear; you create a clear road for the terrorist and for political groups who seek to undermine America's values and principles.

Add the assertion of Islamophobia to the tactics of the left and you can use the BIG LIE against political enemies. If you constantly repeat the lie that Americans are irrationally fearful of Muslims, it is thought, they will come to believe it. What happens when the "chickens come home to roost"? Mr. Awad's final paragraph tells you, "I pray that in the future, this report will be seen as one element in the movement to push back against individuals and institutions who promote hatred and fear of Islam as an American value." Push back? In what way? With what force? For what purpose? How big is this group that must be pushed back and who will do the pushing back? Government, CAIR, Berkeley, terrorists? Will anyone be sent to prison?

Will there be street fights and beatings in the push back?

Who are those individuals and institutions who must be pushed back? The report tells us:

• Pamela Geller and Stop the Islamization of America (SIOA)

• Robert Spencer and Jihad Watch

• Brigitte Gabriel and Act! For America

• Frank Gaffney and the Center for Security Policy (CSP)

• Steven Emerson and the Investigative Project on Terrorism (IPT)

• Newt Gingerich

• The four members of Congress who called for an investigation of Muslim Capitol Hill interns

• Osama bin Laden, Al-Qaeda and other violent extremists

• Daniel Pipes

I'm not going to give you the biographies of these people. You can look them up yourself. However, I will state that most of these people are critics of Islam who draw a connection between the premises of Islam and the justifications used by terrorists for killing Americans. In other words, they are critics of Islam involved in the effort to understand why we were attacked on 9/11/2001. In fact, none of these people appear to fear Islam. There is no evident prejudice in the arguments of these people; most have made a thorough study of Islam and its tenets. And, except for bin Ladin, most of these people are politically conservative.

Yet, the writers of this pamphlet say this:

"A critical study of Islam or Muslims is not Islamophobic," former CAIR Research Director Mohamed Nimer wrote in 2007. "Likewise, a disapproving analysis of American history and government is not anti-American...One can disagree with Islam or with what some Muslims do without having to be hateful."

Try disagreeing with Islam in Saudi Arabia (without being hateful) or in Iran or Syria or Pakistan or any nation dominated by Islam. And try disagreeing with Islam in America without being called Islamophobic by CAIR.

Whom do they consider to be the good people?

• New York Mayor Michael Bloomberg

• Loonwatch (www.loonwatch.com)

• Congressional Tri-Caucus

• Rep. Keith Ellison (a Muslim) (D-MN)

- Jon Stewart, Aasif Mandvi and The Daily Show

- Keith Olbermann and Countdown with Keith Olbermann

- Stephen Colbert and The Colbert Report

- Media Matters for America

- Interfaith Leaders

- Rachel Maddow and The Rachel Maddow Show

This list speaks for itself; but one thing is obvious: Few of these people have ever criticized Islam and some of them are comedians known for making fun of conservatives.

There is no proof that America is a fundamentally racist nation. In fact, America sets the standard for rationality when it comes to judging people according to their characters. Americans, overall, should not feel guilty for their treatment of any group today. The idea of Islamophobia is a concoction of the left intended to impose guilt upon Americans and convince them that they should treat Muslim immigrants differently than they treat American citizens and other immigrants. Rather than analyzing a real issue, offering real solutions that improve society; CAIR and its allies on the left are instead trying to frame the issue to their own political advantage while disregarding true analysis based upon rational standards. They want to politically defeat someone and the key to identifying that someone will tell us much. Who or what do CAIR and Berkeley leftists fear?

A good case can be made for the existence of Ameriphobia in both CAIR and Berkeley. This Ameriphobia is not something new, however. These organizations are grounded in a form of anti-Americanism that has existed since the advent of socialism during the 19th Century. One of the biggest reasons that CAIR and Berkeley are afraid of America is that they accept several myths about our system and those myths are founded, not on reality, but on the views, ideas and fears of the enemies of freedom.

These myths represent a strategy designed to denigrate both capitalism and America in order to set the stage for the lynching of America before the world. The fact that the strategy is not new is an indication that the members of CAIR do not want to foster understanding and fair treatment. They prefer to mimic commonly used fallacies against America to drive a wedge into American society so they can advance their own anti-American agendas.

For instance, in the article from CAIR and Berkeley, you hear no criticism of the violations of individual rights in Iran, about Iran's efforts to destroy Israel and destabilize the Middle East. You hear nothing about Saudi Arabia's efforts to foment jihad around the world and especially in America. You hear nothing about how women and other individuals are being killed and maimed all over the world as an expression of "justice" under Islam. You hear nothing about the racism directed at Jews all over the world but especially in the Middle East. You hear nothing about the riots in the Middle East against Christians or about the treatment of Christians who, in many countries, are not allowed to build churches. You hear nothing about the dictatorships in Iran, Saudi Arabia, Syria, Lebanon and in the Palestinian territories that are destroying the lives of millions of their own citizens. You only hear that America is evil because it is based on self-interest; that it was once a racist country and that it must reform itself and accept anti-Americans as immigrants. And because of the moral implications of anti-capitalism, you seldom hear a protest from American conservatives.

If there are (and I'm sure there are) any truly rights-respecting people within Arab communities in America, they must surely be people who have rejected the barbarism found in their home nations and who have come to America to live as Americans. These people do not like the religious intolerance they have found in their land of birth and they see America as an opportunity to live truly free lives...free of religious dominance and brutality. They come to America to be Americans not Muslims. They don't come to America to hate America. Nor do they fear America.

CAIR thinks that paying lip-service to American values and expressing an opposition to terrorism, will help them fool the American public. They think they can justify their Ameriphobia and anti-Americanism by fighting a long-lived false image of a racist America. One thing is true: you can only hope to get away with this kind of deception with the help of American university professors.

The title of the pamphlet "Same Hate, Different Target" implicates America as fundamentally racist. It is, in essence, an assumption of evil in the American experience by a group of people who both elevate the American experience and seek to bring it down at the same time. It is a statement that America is fundamentally flawed by people who hope to benefit from and exploit the freedoms of America while at the same time destroying those freedoms.

To what "same hate" does the title refer? To the struggle by many whites to win equality for Blacks in America? To the many whites, Asians, Hispanics and blacks who have died for the freedom of oppressed people around the world? To the freedom and economic equality sought by millions of immigrants to America? To the Constitutional protections that have been extended to people of all colors in America? No...the article prefers to focus on the racism in America. That's it...we're a racist nation with a cloud of guilt hanging over us. They call us the oppressors of other nations and we must therefore not be prejudiced and hateful toward them. Instead, we should allow them to institute Sharia Law in America without question.

The title of this document is an insult to Americans. It rings like an insider comment intended only for people who have a particular point of view. It is a statement that would only be made by someone whose ideology contains a strong anti-American bias. Who are the racists according to this ideology? Why, they're conservatives.

The important question to ask is "What happens when you call American free thinking by the name of 'racism'?" You get a political package deal that gives you the ability to call a difference of opinion full-blown racism. It gives you the ability to demonize people who have no racist intent. For instance, in America, if you make a valid point about Christianity from a philosophical perspective, you are not always called anti-Christian. Nor are you called Christian-phobic. But if you say that most racists during the Civil War were Christians, and that this proves all Christians are racists, you are doing a disservice to religion and to Christianity - and you will be roundly criticized for such unfairness. However, this is exactly what CAIR and Berkeley progressives are saying about Americans who happen to disagree with them.

Islam versus America

The cultural clash between Islam and America is not between Christianity and Islam. It is between Islam and freedom. The leaders of CAIR appear to know it. Yet, it is true that Christianity is much more acceptable to the average American than Islam and this is a problem for groups like CAIR who are intent on instituting Sharia Law in America.

Their strategy is to convince Americans that Sharia can exist side-by-side with Constitutional Law and that it does not represent a threat. But this is not true, the two cannot coexist. The cultural clash is too severe and CAIR knows that Sharia Law represents an attitude that can never be accepted in a society that defends individual rights.

Sharia Law assumes that good Muslims must submit to God and that God is government. Islam was established through warfare and it insisted that any conquered people convert to Islam or die. This perspective that Islam is superior to all other religions and all other governments is a direct threat to any nation that has not accepted Islam as government. And, more importantly, in America, it is a direct challenge to the separation of church and state that is vital to our Republic. This conflict can only be resolved by one form of Law superseding the other.

For decades, in America, religion was not allowed into government in order to avoid the tendency of religion to dominate morality and institute religious precepts as mandated practice. The Constitution sought to liberate man from any influence that would circumvent his natural ability to think for himself and it forbade religion from participating in government...even among religious men in government. In other words, religion in America had to accommodate the liberty of man and not seek to impose itself by means of government force. This changed Christianity and made it peaceful. People could be Christian without having to feel that their freedoms were being undermined.

Islam, throughout history, did not have to learn how to "behave" as did Christianity. Most of the nations it influenced were not steeped in the Enlightenment; Islam did not come up against individual rights to the degree that Christianity did; it was not required that it reform itself to survive in secular nations.

Today, Islam has burst upon the scene, without the filtering processes inherent in the Constitution, not as a religion of peace, but as a religion of conquest that considers the secular nature of our society to be decadent, this-worldly and evil. Islam did not have to temper itself to accommodate the Constitution because it gained power by conquest. It feels compelled to destroy any Constitution that would advance secular rights. Throughout history Islam has practiced the ritual of cleansing conquered tribes by forcing other nations to become Muslim. It considers itself to be the true government of man and does not respect the original intent of the Founding Fathers of America to prohibit religion from being the government. It sees this idea as ludicrous because to them Islam is society. Islam is the good.

The result of this approach is not only a disrespect for the principles of America but a belief that America is evil because it has not accepted Islam. Many Muslims see Americans as infidels who sin against God, not because they do truly evil things, but because they live secular lives. The manner of acting that characterizes Americans, their self-assertiveness, their self-confidence, their outspokenness, their way of dress, grooming, their lack of religious piety, even their way of enjoying life, are all problematic for many Imams. These characteristics are considered an insult to God. This is a clash of civilizations for which there can be no compromise. For CAIR, Americans must realize the devout spiritual nature of Islam, see it as superior morally and decide to submit to it. For many Muslims, there is no other choice for America.

Is CAIR using the progressive movement in America as a cover for insinuating Sharia Law? Is it possible that CAIR is asking Americans to consider Islam (a religion that must certainly be in crisis today) as just another group of good citizens who happen to have their own legal system? Is this why Americans are accused of unfairly fearing Islam?

Perhaps the shoe is on the other foot. Islam is in crisis because it seeks to destroy individual rights and there are many secular people who will insist that our society continue to be rooted in the principles of a constitutional republic. Too many Imams fear America because, subconsciously, they know that secular principles have the potential to wipe out fascistic dictatorships. Secular society is much more appealing to Muslims than Islam is appealing to Americans.

The most important consequence of accepting a poorly defined term such as Islamophobia is that it keeps people from acknowledging their justified fears. It blocks intellectually the real fear people have about terrorism, anti-Americanism and hateful lies spouted by religious fanatics, Islamic fascists and progressives alike. For instance, why does CAIR say that conservatives are Islamophobic when they question the actual implications of Islam and, at the same time, why do they say that Americans must stay silent and listen to all forms of criticism in order to avoid being called racist? And further, why are conservatives' questions about Islam considered to be Islamophobic but CAIR's mimicking of progressive criticisms of America considered to be patriotic? The article says,

"Among a certain segment of the population, the Tea-Party and right-wing Republicans, anti-Islam bigotry has become mainstream and lost any taboo. People are unabashed and open in their displays of Islamophobia. In large part, this is in reaction to President Obama's election. Many bigots are upset that we have a black president. But because of the taboo associated with anti-black racism, they are constrained from openly expressing it. So, they falsely declare Obama is a Muslim and feel comfortable denigrating him for that," said a Muslim who has held elected office."

This is an unabashed lie, a repetition of lies told about the Tea Party movement by the left. Another charge made by progressives that black Congressmen were spat upon and endured racist comments during the health care debate was also untrue. Yet, if CAIR claims to be inclusive of all American opinions, why does it make the same baseless political criticisms as the left makes against conservatives? And what are we to think of the many intellectuals who have made reasoned, scholarly arguments that refute the practicability of the progressive policies advanced by President Obama. I'm speaking of classical liberal intellectuals who lived in the 1930s. Were they also racists? How is it that they resented President Obama's blackness before he was born? What are we to think about the people responsible for this report if they are willing to make spurious and false charges such as these?

Remember the list of enemies that CAIR and Berkeley presented in the document? Remember that this list included people and groups that CAIR considered to be Islamophobic. Ask yourself why that list included some conservatives but not the Tea Party movement whose "anti-Islam bigotry has [supposedly] become mainstream". Does this not qualify the movement for that list of Islamophobes? Is it possible that the list was a decoy designed to hide the real enemies who are mainstream Americans? (Brackets mine)

By now the left knows that it is not going to be able to turn the US government into a coercive state without serious opposition. They realize that the Tea Party movement and many conservatives are, to a large extent, a reasoned, principled opposition that will not allow the destruction of the Constitution. They know that there are too many people who understand the reasons and thinking that went into founding our country; too many who understand the meaning of individual rights, and who will not be silenced or steamrolled by invented "emergencies" and outright lies - or by (veiled and open) threats of murder.

Further, organizations like CAIR see the American left as the authors of the cultural diversity ideology that CAIR needs in order to import Sharia Law. They know they must exploit this ideology to succeed; and they know that if Americans reject the concept of cultural diversity, they (CAIR and the left) are in trouble. Americans will not fall for the ploy that a group of people should be allowed to violate the rights of individuals, even those within its group, because of a "divine" law. Americans, for the most part, are decidedly individualistic. They do not consider our nation to be made up of warring collectives vying for control of the government, eager to use government to bash their enemies. Americans, for the most part, judge individuals rationally and encourage individual achievement and freedom. Americanism fights for individuals and because of this, it is an enemy to the numerous collectivists who foster collective solutions, collective sacrifice and collective punishment.

CAIR also knows that American independents and conservatives will not "go silently into the night". They will not submit to Islam and they will not be cowed by statements of collective guilt. Most Americans, because they defend individuals, are naturally opposed to Sharia Law and they will not pretend that accommodations can be made between American jurisprudence, group rock peltings and the exploitation, physical mutilation and abuse of women. To Americans, women are individuals and they cannot be summarily abused and controlled just because a group of men consider themselves to be their masters.

Our nation is moving into dictatorship. But before a dictatorship can take over a country, there must be chaos, violence in the streets and a breakdown of social institutions. This breakdown provides the cover necessary so the coming dictators can jail, imprison and kill political opposition. To accomplish this, the prospective dictators invent "crimes" that the opposition has committed in order to justify destroying them. Today, the left has found a scapegoat in the conservative movement in the same way that the Nazis used the Jews and intellectuals among them, and in the same way that the Soviet communists hated the bourgeoisie and the intellectuals in Russia.

As a participant in the 2009 Tea Party protests, I find it offensive that CAIR and Berkeley claim to be inclusive, while they criticize without basis a group that is made up of the entire demographic of the American populace (conservatives). That CAIR aims its accusations of Islamophobia at people whose issues are budgets and spending should make you wonder at the real issue.

And it is this:

CAIR and Berkeley fear average Americans. They fear us because, as individuals with rights, we are free to think and judge them. They fear us because we represent a very large swath of mainstream America that is descended from the very people who stood up against tyranny and defeated it during the American Revolution. They fear us because they cannot credibly call us ignorant; they cannot declare that we should be ignored and circumvented. They know we won't allow it. Finally, they know that any effort to dictate morality to an American will be met with open disagreement and outright rejection.

Berkeley leftists know that the political strategy of the left is to marginalize the right by unfairly associating anyone on the right with as many negative concepts as possible including the spurious charge of racism. This is a political strategy that apparently CAIR has no problem with, yet it claims to want fairness and openness toward Muslims and other minorities. We know that no one can fight for the rights of some individuals without fighting for the rights of all individuals. There are no group rights.

Most right-leaning intellectuals and even average citizens understand that these tactics are based upon strategies of deception. It is dishonest to demonize political opponents in America by the mere assertion of evil intent. It accomplishes nothing positive and it deflects honest Americans from the important work of solving our very real problems. The left would prefer to play the politics of personal destruction rather than solve problems. Why would CAIR want to be part of this deception?

Where is the Islamophobia in the conservative movement? Our nation was based on a separation of religion and state – and this means all religions, not just Christianity or Islam. Our system was not founded on a disdain for Islam or a desire to limit only Islam. It was founded on a principle that held all religions to be potentially dictatorial. And it was founded on the idea that so long as men did not bring religion into government, they were free to believe any ideas they chose to believe. There is nothing Islamophobic in our system; we do not single out any specific religion when we declare that no religion can impose its views on our nation.

The Founders did not give us their opinions about religion; they gave us principles to help us fight dictatorship. They were not progressives or conservatives; they were individuals. Would they have allowed Sharia Law to exist side-by-side with individual rights? Never – and this is the key: CAIR knows that they can't undermine the Constitution, not now, and maybe never.

The emergence of a principled opposition has put a panic into all progressives and CAIR. They didn't expect that anyone would rise to oppose them. Now they realize that there is a principled movement against them that will not compromise on fundamental principles; and it is a huge movement. They realize that all their arguments for the coercive state no longer work especially the arguments for collectivism and shared sacrifice. They know that eventually they will be swept out of power by this movement in such a large wave that they will be on the outside looking in for the next several generations if not forever. This explains why CAIR and Berkeley kept the Tea Party movement off its list; they didn't want to admit that they feared the movement for liberty more than any other group.

CAIR and Berkeley are participating in political games, picking winners and losers, sticking with the progressives and name-calling (Islamophobe and racist) against one of the largest political groups in the country. Instead of calling for objectivity, refusing to take sides in the political struggle, really meaning what they say about fairness, CAIR chooses instead to get into the political fray and attempt to disenfranchise people who challenge them. CAIR and Berkeley are not fighting Islamophobia; they are exposing their own Ameriphobia.

CAIR and the progressives are doomed to fail. This is because past dictatorships have succeeded in gaining power only by tearing down society and cutting off all lines of communication. Today, that would mean they must destroy mass communication systems such as cable television, the Internet, ebooks, social networking and wireless communications. The freedom that these media rely upon, the freedom of speech, is something Americans are not willing to give up, even if they have no opinion about dictatorship. And, even more importantly, because of its anti-intellectuality, the left has been reduced to a few multi-billionaires who waste huge amounts of money funding failed campaigns and bad ideas. The left needs mass communication in order to multiply by several degrees the amount of drivel they use to drown out the truth.

Altruism

Yet, despite all this, the first "villain" that must be confronted by man is the morality of altruism. Altruism is the first argument made by mystics to disarm their opponents. Altruism holds that morality consists of self-sacrifice. It holds that others are more important than the individual and that the individual should always sacrifice for others rather than do anything for himself.

Religion is the father of altruism. As such, it countenances self-abnegation, self-flagellation and self-hatred. Because it seeks the sacrifice of the human mind to the whims of its leaders, it must necessarily seek the sacrifice of everything. In this regard, it must also dispense tremendous amounts of guilt toward any individual who seeks his own mind, his own thoughts and conclusions.

Altruism was given a modern form by Immanuel Kant who declared that sacrifice (duty) was a moral imperative. Starting with the legacy of the ancient stoics, Kant's philosophy continued the mantra of duty. He insisted that man should hold duty to others above all other acts.

First, Kant facilitated the sacrifice of the human mind by positing two realms, the phenomenal and the noumenal worlds. He deemed the phenomenal world to be a distortion and the noumenal world to be unknowable. In this way, he destroyed man's senses and his mind; leaving men incapable of knowing. In effect, Kant sacrificed the mind in order to make room for God.

Altruism, in its various forms, has been the dominant morality since pre-history and has exerted tremendous influence over man's societies. It is the one key philosophical perspective that has come from pre-history into modern times completely unchallenged. When a mystic issues decrees to the effect that men should sacrifice their property and lives for the sake of a god, they are preaching sacrifice and demanding that men live according to these precepts.

We must not confuse altruism with benevolence or voluntary charity. Although both concepts have similar characteristics (the giver, the middleman and the taker) voluntary charity is based upon the values of the giver whereas altruism is obligatory and often uses force (or moral coercion) to accomplish its goals. Voluntary charity is intended to help specific individuals and can accomplish this goal whereas altruism has no such intent; its goal is to extort goods and other values from enslaved individuals who have no choice about sacrificing for the sake of the collective. Voluntary charity, based upon the giver's values, is "individual" whereas altruism is collective and obligatory.

Many people have yet to recognize the truth that it is altruism, the call to self-sacrifice, that has animated human societies for millennia. Many think that the idea of sacrificing to others has an aura of morality that makes one good. People are inspired by the idea, they want to impress others with their sacrificial acts and they seek to avoid the isolation of ostracism and disfavor that they might receive from society for thinking only of themselves.

But the truth is that altruism is about total slavery and misery for the individual. That is its essence and its goal. Altruism does not seek to improve society; rather it seeks to destroy society and especially success in life. Altruism demands that the best men in society submit to the collective and spend their lives sacrificing and giving to that collective.

The tangible result of altruism is war and genocide, mass murder. Societies such as Nazi Germany, the Soviet Union, Communist China, Communist Cambodia, Communist Cuba, Venezuela represent the examples of societies based upon altruism that felt compelled to kill any individual it deemed an enemy of society. These murdered individuals tended to be the most productive and intelligent people in those societies – and they were cruelly treated and routinely killed because they were productive and intelligent. The numbers of these killed runs into the hundreds of millions – no small number.

These genocides were not aberrations; they were the result of the goals and intents of these societies. These people were killed because of national policy – openly advocated and approved by the leaders and citizens of those countries.

It can be argued that even voluntary charity is a form of altruism. For this, we need to identify a characteristic of both forms that joins them in the same nefarious intents. We can find this characteristic in the concept that living for others is man's highest moral imperative. Voluntary charity is advanced according to this same false notion. Today, innocent people, looking for a moral system to follow, have accepted the notion of voluntary charity as a moral imperative, and in this way, they are advancing the notion that altruism in its more virulent forms is a good morality as well.

The idea of "doing something" to help others seems like a benign idea especially in instances when "helping others" takes place. But the idea of sacrificing one's possessions and life for the sake of a collective tribe or nation has created nearly unspeakable damage to millions of men.

To understand the difference between voluntary charity and sacrifice for the collective, one could say that voluntary charity can be considered the gateway drug which leads eventually to the sacrifice of life and ends with genocide.

The key to avoiding sacrificial genocide is to resist the effort to consider voluntary charity a solution to human problems. It should be viewed as an option that must be tied to human values rather than as a moral imperative. When it is presented as a moral imperative (and when it is accepted as such) then the individual has taken the gateway drug which will eventually destroy his life.

Does this mean that we should refuse to help people who need it and especially people we love or know? No, it does not. The key is to have the proper intellectual approach to altruism by refusing to feel guilty for *not* helping someone. It means also refusing to believe that one is required to help others whenever they have a need.

In a proper society, all individuals are free to advance their own well-being. In such societies, the number of "needy" would be minimal. It is only in societies where plunder (altruism) is the goal (high taxes) that the government impoverishes people in the name of altruism (and thereby creates the needy). In other words, altruism is a self-fulfilling prophesy; it creates the many needy by taking from the productive. The more the productive give, the less they have.

There should be no war against the productive in a society. Properly, the freer an individual, the more productive he becomes and the better society becomes. This diminishes the need for "giving". In short, the answer to altruism is individual rights and capitalism.

Contrast this to the piety that religion demands. The suicide bomber is the perfect example of the evil of altruism. Early in life, he was taught the value of submitting to God and society. He was encouraged to "give" as much as possible to society because this giving would convince god that he deserved heaven. The more he prayed, he thought, the more pious he became, and the closer he was to God. There is very little difference between a man who dies for the sake of violent revolution in society and the man who dies wearing a suicide vest.

The basic mistake of the suicide bombers is that they are giving their life to something that cannot be proven to exist – to a God who was merely asserted to exist by someone who led a questionable life himself. Their insistence that people not question their God or their prophet is a telltale sign that they don't feel certain that God exists. It is not a sign of piety and love but of submission, acceptance and mindlessness.

Altruism, self-sacrifice is a primitive notion developed out of a desire to kill and devastate men. That is why it leads to terrorism, war and genocide. It is the full expression of nihilism, hatred of man and destruction of anything he builds, creates or loves. Altruism is destruction and therefore it's more radical advocates wind up as mindless robots who know only how to kill. They are the dregs of mankind because they have destroyed their own minds through lying to themselves about their own value as slaves to murder.

Men will never be able to defeat terrorism, barbarism and all the destruction they bring about until they realize that self-sacrifice, even in its benign form, contains the epistemological base for the destruction of the good. Until men learn that altruism is evil, base, ugly and hateful, that it hides its ugliness in a maze made up of a pretense to the good, they will never win the struggle for freedom and survival.

It must start in the schools and universities. Someone needs to take on the practitioners of plunder (the progressives) by exposing their real minds, their hatred, their illogic, their base worshipping of the killer that they seek to release upon the earth. It will take a philosophical battle and it will take integrity, logic, clear reasoning and better arguments.

The progressives masquerade as representatives of reason but this is a façade; a lie. As the children of Immanuel Kant, they practice religion every bit as much as the evangelicals that they deride. They pretend to intellectual superiority while they foster skepticism and ridicule of anything that is based upon self-interest, capitalism and individual liberty. They advocate re-distribution of wealth and claim that Marx is scientific. They lie to themselves about the nature of capitalism and they deride the "science" that capitalism demands, claiming that their "science" is unquestionable. They divide society into collectives engaged in social struggles while they struggle to destroy the only economic system that liberates men and leads them to cooperation and peace. They deride individual rights while elevating the criminal and the dictator into positions of revolutionary fighters against exploitation – while they do nothing but murder and exploit.

Today, men are opposed to the fascism of the Nazi Germans. During that period of World War II, men blamed fascism for the murders of the Jews in concentration camps. They did not blame altruism but it was sacrifice for the nation that the Germans extolled and it was this requirement that gives fascism its lethal essence.

Yet, fascism is an economic principle as well and it is being practiced today with the same argument – that men should sacrifice for the sake of the group or nation. Today, our politicians are asking for sacrifice to the collective through re-distribution policies, through tax policies and they incessantly browbeat their political opposition as shills for the exploitation of through capitalism rather than through altruism and sacrifice.

This is their effort to maintain the moral high ground: by preaching the evil of self-interest and the value of self-sacrifice. Even when they lose politically, they never let go of the moral high ground and seek at all costs to maintain it – and they succeed because their political opposition is afraid to stand up for individual rights and self-interest. They feel guilty (as the progressives want them to feel) whenever they stand for capitalist, free market principles and they always capitulate to the progressives.

By the same token, the same moral high ground is assumed by mystics of virtually every religion as they admonish man and threaten him with eternal punishment should they refuse to sacrifice for the collective. The radical Muslims (jihadists) assume the same position when they insist that they have the right to act like gangsters and kill anyone, even people of their own religion, for refusing to submit to their God. They are so consistent in these positions that those among the opposition to the progressives have little to say. How can one fight against this kind of extreme religious piety? How can one fight against people who "believe" so strongly that God wants them to impose their views (by means of force) on everyone?

It is time to stop capitulating to altruism. It is time to start extolling the value of individual freedom and capitalism. It is time to stop feeling guilty for advocating individualism and true morality. The advocates of altruism are not defending morality but destroying the possibility of it. It is time to take them (progressives and mystics) to task for advocating the destruction of individual lives and their property. It is time to stop "believing" that altruism represents the good – it does not.

The answer to mysticism and altruism requires more than merely rejecting these ideas. The key is reason and its consistent use. The key is the defense of human values by means of logic and clear thinking. We should never countenance faith and the suspension of reason. Indeed, mysticism and altruism require the wholesale suspension of reason and, because this is so, they require the destruction of rational thought and understanding. We must fight for reason if we are to defeat murderous monsters who prey upon the weak-minded people they call to submission.

Mysticism, altruism and collectivism are the enemies of reason, self-interest and individual rights[1]. These are clear divisions that separate progressives from freedom-loving individuals. Progressivism elevates only skeptics, communists, progressives and religious mystics. Against them are people who advocate reason, individualism and representative republican government. In short, the division is between tyranny with oppression and liberty with individual rights.

The superiority of reason over mysticism is the key difference between those who love America and those who hate it. Mystics fear reason and likewise

---

[1] I credit Ayn Rand with first identifying these principles.

they fear America and its superiority. They have a visceral response to the idea of independent individuals who think for themselves and America is the prime example of a nation of independent individuals. They have a subliminal fear of any nation that is efficacious and successful compared to their failures and incompetence. This is the source of Ameriphobia. America is fearful to them because it demands that they stand up and be responsible for themselves. It is this idea that they fight with every breath of their poisonous and nonsensical rationalizations. Will they go to heaven? Hell no.

A free and independent people do not fear any form of mysticism – if they are left free. They have no reason to think that mysticism has any grasp on the real world. Mystics are failures at living and because so, there is nothing to fear about them. Their only power is in the acceptance that free individuals allow; the moral equivalence they give to mysticism. Once men break the vicious cycle of unwarranted equivalence between mysticism and reason, there will be nothing to fear.

Conclusion

Holding secular society responsible for evil in the world is a false quest. Everyone is responsible for his own actions and each of those actions should be based upon the self-interest of the individual. They are good or bad based upon their effect on the individual's life and that of others. To accuse an individual of self-interest for pursuing his own interests; and calling this evil is itself an evil act. It encroaches on the rights that everyone owns.

If radical mystics want to purify the earth by offering a murderous philosophy to honest men, they will surely lose. Eventually, free men will recognize the impracticability of the idea of secular evil and they will respond appropriately to murderous criminals.

The key for people living in countries dominated by ideas that countenance murder is for them to reject wholesale their murderous philosophies. To be truly innocent, they must accept the truth that the best kind of society is a secular society that separates religion and government; that individual rights are the key to proper society and that everyone is autonomous and capable of living successfully and in peace. These Islamic societies must accept capitalism as a statement of these principles in action. The battle against mysticism is a battle for life and peaceful living. The battle can be won if we stand up for freedom and refuse to compromise with those who want to kill us.

Islamophobia is a wholly concocted hatred. And this is the crux of the matter. Likewise, Ameriphobia is based upon a false belief that free societies are exploitative and evil. There is nothing about America to fear if one is an honest actor. America is the beacon of freedom for anyone suffering under the yoke of socialism, communism and religious bigotry. America is the answer to dictatorship and especially, it is the answer to Islam; a religion that is in crisis.

However, if one is a dictator who seeks to exploit his people; if one is a religious bigot who seeks to enslave mankind for the sake of "piety" and love of god; if one is a communist who seeks violent revolution; then one will fear America as the dispenser of justice against injustice. And this is why so many Imams hate America.

In this context, then, one must reject the views of American progressives and college professors who also rail against America and imperialism. How is it that they have advocated opposition to "conservatism" when they bask in the freedom of speech that the U. S. Constitution defends? Why do these men hate and fear individual rights while they rely on their protection in the society in which they live?

Honest observers of this clash of civilizations must recognize that the two fundamental points of opposition in the world are individual rights versus dictatorship. In the guise of morality and "good living" the radical Islamists seek to take over the world by insisting that man submit his choices, actions and allegiances to a spiritual entity that has no reality. One cannot rationalize this fact out of existence.

A great deal of intellectual work needs to be done before the world can begin to reject Islamic fascism and foster individual rights. But it is important to note that human progress, the advance of better ideas, can only lead to the rejection of philosophical systems that foster the violation of individual rights. Medieval dictatorships with their rampant wars, monarchical power lust, cruelty and murder cannot represent the advance of civilization. It has come down to this: destruction or civilization. Anyone who seeks to offer destruction as a solution for man today is an enemy of man, a nihilist who seeks the destruction of mankind and his societies.

If we advocate individual rights and want to ensure the existence of a secular society, then we must begin to argue against the false claims about capitalism, secularism and free societies. We must divorce profit-seeking, moral freedom and republican government from the false criticisms of the mystics, the Marxists and the progressives. We need to expose their arguments as pseudo-arguments that do not reflect the real world. And we should show them why secular society is the only hope for morality and moral living.

This will take time but we must begin the conversation or radicals and terrorists will win by default; tyranny, genocide and fascism will have no opposition. Let us vow to never allow our voices for freedom to be drowned out by deception and malice.